A Gift
of Prayer

❖

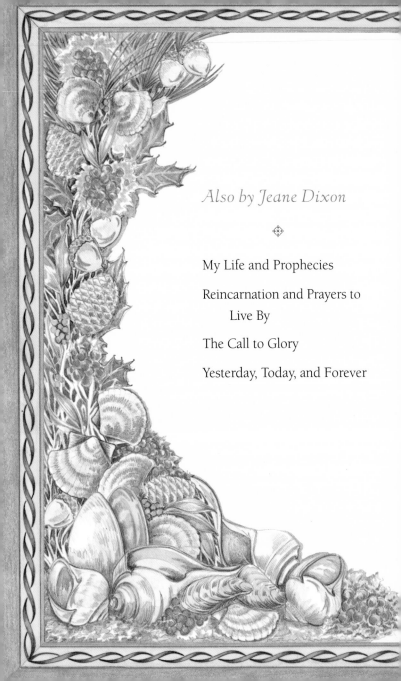

Also by Jeane Dixon

✧

My Life and Prophecies

Reincarnation and Prayers to
   Live By

The Call to Glory

Yesterday, Today, and Forever

A Gift
of Prayer

❖

Words of Comfort and
Inspiration from the Beloved
Prophet and Seer

❖

Jeane Dixon

WATERCOLORS BY LAUREN JARRETT

VIKING
STUDIO
BOOKS

VIKING STUDIO BOOKS
Published by the Penguin Group
Penguin Books USA Inc., 375 Hudson Street,
New York, New York 10014, U.S.A.
Penguin Books Ltd, 27 Wrights Lane, London W8 5TZ, England
Penguin Books Australia Ltd, Ringwood, Victoria, Australia
Penguin Books Canada Ltd, 10 Alcorn Avenue,
Toronto, Ontario, Canada M4V 3B2
Penguin Books (N.Z.) Ltd, 182–190 Wairau Road,
Auckland 10, New Zealand

Penguin Books Ltd, Registered Offices:
Harmondsworth, Middlesex, England

First published in 1995 by Viking Penguin,
a division of Penguin Books USA Inc.

1 3 5 7 9 10 8 6 4 2

Grateful acknowledgment is made for permission to reprint the
prayer by Dr. Benjy Brooks appearing on page 29.
Used by permission of Dr. Brooks.

LIBRARY OF CONGRESS CATALOGING IN PUBLICATION DATA
Dixon, Jeane.
A gift of prayer: words of comfort and inspiration from
the beloved prophet and seer / Jeane Dixon;
watercolors by Lauren Jarrett.
p. cm.
ISBN 0-670-86010-7
1. Prayer—Christianity. 2. Prayer. I. Title.
BV215.D58   1995
242'.8—dc20   95-9012

Printed in Singapore
Set in Italian Electric and Berkeley Book
Slipcase, cover and interior design by Kathryn Parise

In immortal memory of
JAMES LAMB DIXON,

most loving and beloved husband,
wisest of counsellors, lifetime leader in
our household prayer, eternal inspiration of
my life, more vivid with each new day

AND

To my sister,
EVELYN (PINKY) BRIER,

extraordinary pioneer of the air, whose
exploration of the heavens opened a pathway of
divine light; who is a source of great strength
as companion in this world and by her prayers
an incomparable friend before the
gates of heaven

AND

To CAPUCINE,
for her love and fierce loyalty

My heartfelt appreciation goes out first and foremost to Norma Langley, my partner in prayer, who has so faithfully fulfilled the important role as editor as well as friend; and to Candace Carell, fellow worker dedicated to God's undying vineyard who shares credit for the sweet fruit and immortal vintage of prayer.

The prayers in this book have been inspired by so many, whether still living among us or eternally delighting in the Lord. All of their names are forever written in letters of gold upon my heart. God's greatest gifts to all His children are the spirits with whose sweetness He fills our lives. I am forever grateful for them and to them.

Contents

✢

A Gift
of Prayer

❖

Come Pray
with Me

*All things, whatsoever ye shall ask in
prayer, believing, ye shall receive.*
—MATTHEW 21:22

The longer I live, the more I realize that, along with the gift of prophecy, I have been blessed with the gift of prayer. And of the two, the one that is more central to my life is prayer.

Without my prayer life, there could be no prophecy. Prayer is both the preparation and the thanksgiving for my prophecies. Prophecies mark the rare occasions when the heavens remind us that God speaks to each generation.

We know from ancient legend, as well as from recorded history, that God picks prayerful people in every age and nation to carry His message. But occasions of prophecy are like love—to some, they come only once in a lifetime.

The rare occurrences of prophecy in my life were never under my control. Whenever I experienced a prophetic message, I tried to make clear that nothing I did made me worthy of it, nothing I did willed it into being, and nothing I could do would effect a change in the message.

I am ever mindful of the warning of the apostle Matthew, who called such gifts something that "You received without paying" (Matthew 10:8).

Prayer, on the other hand, is ours to claim every day of our lives. In the second it takes to think, "God, help me!" we have prayed. If we open our minds for another second, hoping for inspiration to meet the challenge, we have meditated.

Prayer, which includes meditation, is my ongoing dialogue with God. It is comforting, enlightening, and fills a hunger of the mind and spirit in a way that nothing else can touch.

I pray believing that God will answer. To hear or feel His answer, the chatter of the mind must be quieted. Prayer-meditation is the invitation for God to take over. At times, during meditation, I hear a whisper of a voice within. And then comes a feeling that if I follow that voice all will be well.

How to begin a conversation with God? A good start is to do as we have been told! All of our lives, the prayers we learned as children comfort the child that lives on in each of us.

The prayers of youth have a way of coming back to us. I believe I have heard the prayer "Glory be to the Father, the Son, and the Holy Spirit" every day of my life. And on many days I hear the beautiful prayers of my neighbors affirming their faith: "There is no God but Allah!" "Hear, O Israel, the Lord our God, the Lord is One." Your faith may use other affirmations, but I have no doubt there are prayers of praise for some higher power in your mind and heart.

While every religious heritage has powerful prayers of praise, God has also inspired us to ask for His help. A prayer like the Lord's Prayer is a model of praise and petition for our daily needs, including protection from evil.

4

THE LORD'S PRAYER

Our Father, Who art in heaven, hallowed be Thy name; Thy kingdom come; Thy will be done on earth as it is in heaven. Give us this day our daily bread; and forgive us our trespasses as we forgive those who trespass against us; and lead us not into temptation, but deliver us from evil.

The words that conclude the prayer vary from person to person; but no matter what we say, our own words are just as dear to God as those composed by saints and churchmen.

Early each morning I try to offer something to God before I begin praying for my own benefit. For instance, when I say, and really mean, "Lord, I dedicate this day to You," I feel I've invited a friend to spend the day with me.

A prayer of praise also does wonders for me upon rising; it gives me rest from yesterday's troubles. It gives me hope that God will help me through a day that may include pain, fear, or disappointment. "Thank God!" is a much better start for any day than "Woe is me!"

All who have grieved know there are days when praise comes hard to mind.

Whenever I need help finding the words, I think of St. Francis of Assisi, who was in poor health and nearly blind when he praised God with unbounded joy in the "Canticle of Brother Sun." St. Francis taught us that there is always reason to give thanks for being born into the world God created for us.

THE CANTICLE OF BROTHER SUN

. . . .

All praise be yours, my Lord, through all that
you have made,
   And first my lord Brother Sun,
   Who brings the day; and light you give to us
   through him.

. . . .

All praise be yours, my Lord, through Sister
Moon and Stars;
   In the heavens you have made them, bright
   And precious and fair.
All praise be yours, my Lord, through Brothers
Wind and Air,
   And fair and stormy, all the weather's
   moods,
   By which you cherish all that you have
   made.

All praise be yours, my Lord, through Sister
Water,
   So useful, lowly, precious, and pure.

All praise be yours, my Lord, through Brother
Fire,
   Through whom you brighten up the night.

A taste of prayer and meditation in the morning whets the appetite for more. But how much more are we to do? The answer is in St. Paul's instructions to the Thessalonians: "Pray without ceasing!"

Like all who value prayer, I send up entreaties to God all through the day. "God, don't let me forget I have the stove on. . . . Dear God, let me say the right thing. . . . Oh God, where did I put my glasses?" Seemingly capricious, these prayers reveal an unspoken surrender to God's will. This, I believe, is good and real prayer based on a lifetime of friendship with God.

When you make prayer central to your life, prayers of desire fly heavenward all day and, sometimes, all night long. Prayerful people expect these prayers will be answered. When they are, often we forget that we have prayed. I trust in God's forgiveness when I neglect to say "thank you" to him—because I am too busy congratulating myself on solving the problem.

Even if the answer to prayer is "no," and we must give up what we seek, there is comfort. No prayer is lost. It has flown from your lips to God's ear and someday,

in His good time, we will know He remembers each of our smallest prayers.

Recently I took a tumble and broke a hip. I found then that in desperate times, distress is a great mind-focusing device.

What does one pray for in such times? For me, relief from pain was the first thought, but a good orthopedic doctor was what I really needed—and what God knew I needed.

Surgery corrected the problem, but as I lay waiting for help I knew the power of God—the creative force that gives you the strength to bear pain. I know that if God had wished it so, He could have healed me with faith alone. And I know too that God, in answer to my prayers, guided the surgeon's hand who fixed my hip.

The answer to my prayer, thank God, was yes! But in His way, in His time, not mine.

The gift of prayer is everyone's birthright. Prayer was born with God's first breath into Adam and Eve. Like us, they were creatures made to receive His love. Their prayers of praise for life in Paradise surely turned to prayers for forgiveness when they sinned and felt the first harsh winds blow upon their nakedness.

Prayer blossomed when God revealed himself to ancient prophets like Abraham. He passed his knowledge of God on to his progeny, who in turn built the Muslim, Jewish, and Christian faiths.

How good it is to know that the God of our fathers made heaven, earth, and the stars above!

The Joy of Knowing

In accomplishing our mission, teach us to treat the affairs of the world with a real sense of Christian responsibility and a joyful hope of the coming of God's Kingdom, and of a "new heavens and a new earth."

—POPE JOHN PAUL II

Knowing is wisdom. Knowing is understanding that God calls us by name, sees our creation and our end, and loves each of us enough to write the script of our lives.

If there is one prayer that can challenge us and bring us joy, it is this:

Lord, make me according to Thy heart.
—BROTHER LAWRENCE, BORN
NICHOLAS HERMAN; 1611–1691

The desire to fulfill our destiny to the highest degree is universal and makes brothers and sisters of us all.

God promised Jeremiah a plan for his lifetime: "They are plans for good and not for evil, to give you a future and a hope."

I believe that knowing when we are realizing our highest potential is the main ingredient of peace. And following God's plan brings the truest and most enduring happiness we will experience on earth.

To give thanks and protect my joy, I pray:

Search me, O God, and know my heart; test my thoughts. Point out anything you find in me that makes You sad, and lead me along the path of everlasting life.
—PSALM 139:23–24

Knowing we are guided by a higher power is precious whenever it comes to us. For many, day-to-day signs are elusive. For some, knowing is a gift saved for the twilight of life, when we look back at children reared or battles won. Blinders fall from older eyes once we no longer strive for power, possessions, or the excitement of falling in love.

For some lucky few, the precious gift of knowing God's plan comes sooner. Joan of Arc knew in her teens that God called her to lead the armies of the French. Moses was only a baby when he was floated into Egypt to prepare himself to lead his people to the promised land.

But knowing is not just a gift for young saints and Old Testament prophets. They were summoned by heaven-sent bolts of self-knowledge. Most of us receive our gift of knowing through prayer.

One of the most fulfilled people I've ever met was a stonemason. He spent his youth learning his father's art and praying to his heavenly father for a cathedral. At last he was called to sculpt animals and saints for the world's only cathedral under construction. He moved his family from Italy and began a new prayer—that work on the National Cathedral in Washington, D.C., would last his lifetime. Again his prayer was answered. God's plan and the man's acceptance made for a rich and happy life.

✣

Prayer for True Vocation

Dear Lord, as I know You created me,
*   as I know You call me by name,*
I also know that You have written the script for
*   my life among the stars.*
My fulfillment is there for the finding,
and I know what I must do.
I ask You now to reveal my work in Your vine-
*   yard.*
Reveal how my existence can justify a place in
*   heaven and satisfy my needs on earth.*
Reveal Your plan for me and only me.
Open my Heart to hear Your voice.
Show me my true vocation,
So that I may find peace in doing Your will.

I count myself among the blessed who heard a call early in life. I don't remember a moment of childhood when I was unaware of a mission and purpose that had to be obeyed no matter what the cost.

Like all faith, knowing is constantly challenged by life's little setbacks. We lose a job, break a leg, come home to find we've been robbed. We feel ourselves slipping backward, rather than going forward.

Even success challenges knowing.

Then we ask ourselves: Did we aim too low, were we aiming in the wrong direction? Did we truly hear the word of God or only the voice of our own ambition? In this twilight of confusion, we cry out the universal prayer: *"Dear God, is this all there is?"*

To me, that heartbroken prayer that springs from our lips unbid is a small divine mystery.

No one ever had to be taught the words, "Is this all there is." Our hearts beseech our Father in heaven to help us start over.

Who among us has not yearned for a better life, or a chance to leave some sign that we have lived, loved, and tried to make the lives of others better for knowing us?

14

The divine mystery is this. Who but God programmed that phrase into each human heart so that sooner or later we would fall to our knees and acknowledge our need for His love?

If the trials and errors of my own life are an example, knowing does not keep us from making mistakes along the way. Each day brings a new battle to harness the ego, which is the wild child of free will.

Free will brings spiritual growth only when we choose the most honorable choices before us. The way to harness an inflated ego is to make no important decision without first consulting with God through prayer:

Prayer for Guidance

Lord, I am lost. I have tried to make my life more pleasing to You. I am looking for the peace of knowing I am doing the best I can. I will clear my mind and open my heart to Your guidance and Your love.

It takes patience to wait, however long it takes, to hear that still small voice within that always answers this prayer. God *always*, sooner or later, answers sincere prayer.

But, if in answer, I hear nothing but my own advice, I know I must finish the prayer:

Your Will, Lord, not mine
in Your good time, Lord, not mine.

Knowing, like all wisdom, ultimately lights the darkness left by life's losses. Knowing we are fighting the good fight, or have fought it, is comforting. Knowing we are following the script written by the Lord at our conception is peace.

The more we pray to know God's plan for our lives, the closer we come to living it and reaping our joy.

When I know the Lord has spoken, I am filled with joy.

PRAYER OF KNOWING

I am never without You. With each passing year the words of scripture ring more true: Your angels do watch over us. Working late into the night, working early in the mornings before dawn, I am so much of the time alone, but I am never lonely. In the stillest and darkest hours I hear Your angels around me, bringing the music of the spheres from heaven to earth.

Each day is Your gift to us, which we return to You at its sleepy conclusion. Our life is likewise Your gift, which we each give back in due time. It is not possible to enfold my whole life in glorious wrapping and brilliant ribbon, but I can decorate each day with dedicated work and dwell in Your spirit.

And then, dear God, when all my days are put together, what a splendid package they will make! Please accept them as my thanksgiving gift for the joy of finding myself, and knowing!

❖

Praying for Children

Verily I say unto you,
inasmuch as ye have done it
unto one of the least of
these my children, ye
have done it unto me.
—MATTHEW 25:40

The moment a child comes into our arms for the first time must be the closest we can come to heaven on earth. Participating as parents in God's creation of a new life is as sacred as the priesthood; more love-filled than any other human endeavor.

Parenthood is a call to prayer that lasts from the moment a girl or boy thinks ahead in life to establishing a family until the final breath of life.

There may be no more pleasing prayer to God than "Bless our union with a child." Such a prayer rises from loving hearts ready to accept parenthood as the highest calling of their lives.

The covenant or contract involved in bringing a child into the world is highly sacred, for we become caretakers of a unique and precious soul.

Bless Our Union with a Child

Dear Lord, love like ours is meant to be shared. We are ready to show our love for You and for each other by conceiving a child. We promise to love, honor, and cherish a child as a part of a family that is pleasing to You. Lord, we yearn for this child from the deepest recesses of our hearts. We can wait, but we pray Your answer will come soon. Bless our union with a child. If it is Your will, send a new and precious soul to us. Here is

19

my promise, Lord: I will love the child You send me, and I will teach my child to love You.

For those who yearn for children, or need guidance in raising children, there is no greater hope or comfort than in prayer.

But our prayers for parenthood, like every other gift we ask of God, must be uttered with humble and accepting hearts. I believe that God chooses those who cannot bear a child with as great a love as He chooses those who will bear many children.

To nurture a child is among the highest callings of both men and women. I have heard the heartbreak of both when their desires are not fulfilled.

In those cases, perhaps, as in my own, God has other plans.

One of the first visions I ever had revealed was that I must use my psychic abilities to do something for children. At the same time, it was also understood that there would be no special child to accept my love as a mother. In other words, God gave me a garden to tend, but not one single flower to call my own. And with that I have been content.

In the Catholic faith, we believe that Mary taught us the perfect prayer of acceptance of God's will. Confirmed with motherhood before she was a wife, Mary, who was pure, faced total disgrace. Yet when the angel

Gabriel told her she was blessed among women, she had the grace to say:

Behold, the handmaid of the Lord. Be it unto me according to Your word.

—Luke 1:38

What I know of parenting comes from observation and the thousands of letters I have received asking for psychic guidance. Through the years, I've augmented my psychic "feelings" for the families who put their trust in me by seeking advice from experts in medicine and psychiatry.

Strangely enough, I found that my own parents were wiser than we appreciated as we grew up under their loving care. Frank and Emma Pinckert lived with faith in God and love for their adopted country, America. Through them, I learned that children are taught by example, not by mere words.

Prayer and loving discipline were as natural to my family as food and water. Among the first prayers I said with my mother was this one:

LORD OF TREES AND FLOWERS

Dear Lord, Who made the trees and flowers,
Thank You for all the happy hours
I have spent in play and learning.
Now the stars of night are burning
Like Your lanterns in the sky.
The birds are sleeping. So shall I.

You care for every web and wing,
Protecting every little thing:
Puppy, kitten, birdie, bee.
O keep them safe, and please bless me!

My parents taught us that expressing our gratitude to
God was a daily responsibility. At mealtimes we prayed:

PRAYER OF THANKSGIVING

Thank You for the earth so sweet,
Thank You for the food we eat,
Thank You for the birds that sing,
Thank You, God, for everything.

Then each of us was invited to add our own special word of praise or need. We trusted each other to respect these prayers, since the idea of voicing prayers at the table comes from God's promise that "where two or three are gathered together in my name, there I am in the midst of them" (Matthew 18:20). To mock another's prayer was to mock the tradition of our family and God's presence among us. We understood that our place at the table was earned through respect—giving as much consideration to each other as we hoped to get in return.

I hear those childhood prayers now in my memory. They were pure little wishes—beautiful intercessions for the good of the family.

LET ME PRAY AS A CHILD

Lord, let me capture the pure spirit of a loving
child when I speak Your name.
Let me pray as a child prays, asking little for
myself, much for other souls and for Your
beautiful world.
Protect me, sleeping and waking, from evil.
Lead me by the hand to good works.
Let me praise You in simple words and in
glorious silence
through all the days and the nights of my life.

23

As children, we accepted prayer as part of daily life. In my parents' house, we heard our father pray for easy birth of cattle and a good harvest. We heard our mother pray for jams to set and for childhood illnesses to pass.

Nothing starts a parent praying like the illness of a beloved child. My mother taught me that God has His reasons for allowing illness and pain in the world, and I often heard her beg the Lord to transfer pain from her child to herself.

My mother knew that some children come as gifts. Some stay just for a little while. But she also believed, as I do, in miracles. The scriptures tell us that the Lord can raise the dead, cure the sick, and drive out the demon.

Many nights both Mother and Father stood by the bed of a sick child, praying. Who is so bereft of hope that he will not pray for a child?

Prayer for a Suffering Child

Dear Lord, this child who is here before You
      suffers from pain I cannot heal.
If I could take the pain upon myself, I would.
Yet deep in my heart
I know that is not Your way.
Your miracles are beyond the small gift of my
      suffering.
Instead You require faith of me.
The faith of Elijah when he called
You to raise up a little boy. The faith that cured
      the son of a nobleman.
The faith of Jarius when he begged Jesus to
      raise his daughter from the dead.
How often You, our hope, have triumphed over
      death and suffering.
Yet we know suffering is a part of life, and if it
      must be so, let it go lightly with this child.
I put my treasure in Your hands.
Help me, Lord, to get my baby, Your finest gift
      to me, through the night.

A parent's prayer as a child grows is an embodiment of filial love. It is a prayer that God's strength will carry the child away to a happy life of his own.

Let This Child Fly
with an Angel of Wisdom

Dear Lord, let me put my dreams for my precious child in Your hands. Let me love enough to let my child reach for his own dreams. Let me love enough to let this child fly.

But Lord, no child can fly alone. There is too much temptation and trouble in this world. Send this special child of mine an angel of wisdom who will whisper Your word into a youthful ear. Give my child the faith to listen even when it means he must break away from the comfort of earthly acceptance.

In time, character and faith will grow. The spirit of youth will combine with wisdom so that your name will be praised through a new generation.

We do not push children toward faith, we lead them. They do the pushing from the moment they utter their first spontaneous prayer: "Why can't I see God?"

What can you answer? That God is spirit, not body. That we don't see God, but know God through faith. That feeling God as a spirit of love is the most important use of human senses.

The great reward of parenting, to grow in faith with a child's precious soul, is universal to all religions.

About twenty-five years ago, I helped raise some money for an Indian school. As I was about to leave the reservation, a Sioux mother handed me a prayer. How long this prayer has been handed down in Sioux families, I do not know. But surely God is revealed in these lines:

Prayer to the Great Spirit

O Great Spirit, whose voice I hear in the winds and whose breath gives life to all the world, hear me! I am small and weak, and I need your strength and wisdom.

Let me walk in beauty, and make my eyes ever behold the red and purple sunset. Make my hands respect the things you have made and my ears sharp to hear your voice.

Let me learn the lesson you have hidden in every leaf and rock.

I seek strength, not to be greater than my brother, but to fight my greatest enemy—myself.

Make me always ready to come to you with clean hands and straight eyes.

So when life fades, as the fading sunset, my spirit may come to you without shame.

Children have been a big part of my life's work. With the first money I made as a lecturer more than thirty years ago, I established the Children to Children Foundation for perinatal research.

One of the outstanding doctors who has worked with me through the years is Dr. Benjy Brooks. Dr. Brooks, formerly chief of pediatrics at Houston's Hermann Hospital, now plies her surgical skills for Children to Children in Romania. This is Dr. Brooks's prayer:

Dear Lord—O great physician—give me the skill I need with my hands to make this baby whole again. Give me clear vision and judgment to make the right decisions.

Bring Your comfort to this baby's mother and father. Relieve their anxiety as they wait. Be close to the grandparents and all who love this life that You have given.

With the simple faith of a child I rely on You.

My Five Angels

Lord, send an angel of peace, a faithful guide, a guardian of our souls and bodies.

—Eastern Orthodox prayer

In a moment of danger, when I was a child, I was saved by five angels.

It happened in a barn where my father kept horses. In that barn there were many wonderful places to play hide-and-seek and to practice feats of daring.

I'd seen my big brother, Ernie, jump from beam to beam. It seemed so easy and so much fun. It didn't occur to me that a brother who would go on to become a college All-American and a professional football player might be better equipped for rafter jumping than a small girl.

While Ernie was busy climbing down a ladder on one side of the barn after his romp, I was busy climbing up the ladder on the opposite side. My first stop was a wide loft running six feet out from the wall all around the barn. In the middle were open rafters.

Up close, the rafters looked much farther apart than they had from the safety of the floor. My brother saw me as I was about to leap and yelled, "Don't do it!"

Too late—I was airborne.

From down below, Ernie saw a quick and perfect landing on the first rafter, then another and another until I reached solid footing on another loft at the far end of the barn. I had sailed across about six open rafters, each perhaps two feet apart. Ernie told me afterward that he thought I was flying.

But for me, up on the rafters, time stood still. I realized that my legs were just too short to reach from rafter to rafter. There was a moment of regret that Ernie would see me fall. Then absolute delight returned. I saw angels more beautiful than any in a picture book. And then I felt them—an angel for each hand and foot and another set of wings beneath me.

For some reason, I was not surprised. There were no words spoken, but I felt a sense of love and anticipation—as if I'd always known these five magnificent creatures. It was my first taste of ecstasy. Those friendly angels saw me safely onto the ladder, and although they faded from sight when I reached the ground, I knew they were still with me, and would always be with me.

Most people are aware of the protection provided by angels. But there is so much more.

Exodus 23:20–21 tells us:

"Behold I send an angel before thee, to keep thee in the way and to bring thee into the place which I have prepared. Beware to him and obey his voice."

Angels help us recognize spiritual road signs. And the older we get, the more we should open ourselves to the help angels can give us in one important quest—to recognize God's truth. That is why many religions have called angels "messengers." Remember their message to the Bethlehem shepherds: "Peace to men of good will."

Your guardian angel has the same power today to open your heart to the truth and peace if you listen.

But remember that we do not pray to angels—we pray to God to have them assigned to our service. Sometimes we call on our special angels to speed a prayer to God.

Christians, Jews, Muslims, and American Indians all have angelic traditions.

The prophet Mohammed taught that every raindrop is accompanied by an angel. There is also a lovely story in the Jewish tradition that a guardian angel visits us just before we are born, touching our upper lip, whispering to us not to tell what we know about heaven. And that is why we are born with a little cleft above our lips.

It was revealed in the Old Testament that St. Michael, the Archangel, was made protector of Israel. His was the sword of God in the great confrontation with the forces of Lucifer. From the beginning of recorded history, soldiers of many faiths have called upon him in prayer to "defend us in battle."

Muslims honor Gabriel as the angel who appeared to the prophet Mohammed in mountain caves near Mecca. In like spirit, Gabriel appeared to the maiden Mary, hailing her as the chosen of God to bear Christ for the world.

The Archangel Raphael will trumpet on the Last Day, according to Muslim belief. Many believe Raphael is the chief of guardian angels. Christians and Jews honor Raphael as inspiration for healing.

Muslims take special note of the Angels Kirman and Kathibeen, recorders of good and bad deeds. And once the trumpet has sounded, the angels Munkar and Nakir will greet those who have risen on the Last Day.

Angels inspire beautiful thoughts. Two that always come to my mind are: There is room enough in the heart of man for many angels, for angels take no room. And: The music of the angels keeps the universe in motion.

My personal belief in angels is so strong that I have never felt totally alone in my life. I have traveled alone. I have mourned loved ones, survived accidents, known fear. But my angels are always there to comfort, protect, and enlighten.

Whether you have been assigned one or a dozen, your personal angels are with you right now—never too busy or too tired to stand at your side, helping you to send your needs to the ear of God in prayer and to speed His wisdom to you.

A simple old Eastern Orthodox prayer teaches us how to pray for the company of angels: "Lord, send an angel of peace, a faithful guide, a guardian of our souls and bodies."

Because I first experienced angels as life savers, I automatically ask God to speed my special angels to me in times of danger or illness:

LEND ME A BAND OF ANGELS

Dear Lord, I am afraid. If you will, surround me quickly with the protection of angels who have the strength to move mountains. Lend me a band of angels to help my gentle guardians in this time of need. My trust is in You, Lord, Who command as many angels as there are raindrops. But if it is my time, let the angels lead me to heaven.

Sometimes a psychic flash tells me that a friend is in immediate danger. If I cannot get a warning through in time, I know I can ask God to speed angels to protect anyone, anyplace in the world.

Often I find out how these stories end—listening to tales of near misses. There are blessings to be gathered even if the friend didn't recognize angelic intercession. Lives can be changed dramatically by such solid proof of God's love.

LORD, SEND THE POWERFUL

Dear Lord, send help. And if possible send it now. Send a company of angels to protect my friend from fear or illness. Send the powerful to defend the powerless. I know not what future You decree for my dear one, but I cry out for protection from unnecessary suffering. I see danger moving close, but I am unable to help. All I can do is put my trust in You and the protection of a band of invulnerable angels. Lend them to us in our hour of need.

35

Prayers for the comfort of angels are part of many traditions. Children of many countries love this daily communication with their guardian angel:

Angel of God, my guardian dear
to Whom His love commits me here
ever this day be at my side
to light and guard, to rule and guide.

This beautiful entreaty comes from the Anglican *Book of Common Prayer*:

O everlasting God, who hast ordained and con-
stituted the services of angels and men in won-
derful order; Mercifully grant, that as Thy holy
angels always do Thee service in heaven, so by
Thy appointment they may succor and defend us
on earth.

This prayer was written by Pope Leo XII, who was inspired by a vision of a fearful battle between Satan and St. Michael:

Prayer for St. Michael

St. Michael the Archangel, defend us in the day of Battle; be our safeguard against the wickedness and snares of the Devil. May God rebuke Him, we humbly pray, and do Thou, O Prince of the Heavenly Host, by the power of God, cast into Hell, Satan and all the other evil spirits who prowl through the world, seeking the ruin of souls.

When whatever danger we fear is past, as it must certainly pass, we should thank the Lord and ask Him to release our extra band of angels.

Prayer of Thanksgiving for Angels

Lord, thank You for my angels, who have never failed me. Let me be conscious of them in any good works that I do. Give them the joy of carrying my praise to Your ear and laying each small offering at Your throne.

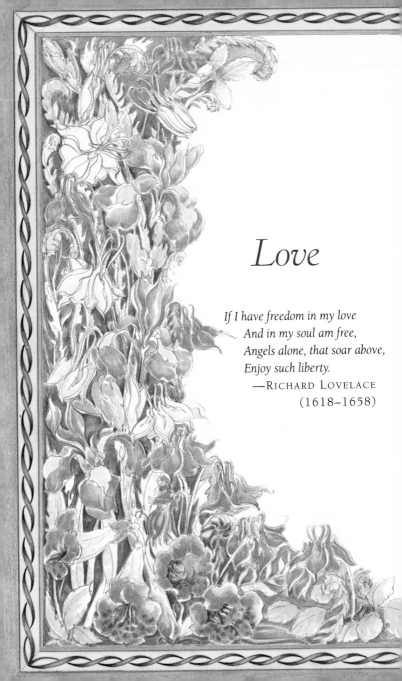

Love

If I have freedom in my love
And in my soul am free,
Angels alone, that soar above,
Enjoy such liberty.
—RICHARD LOVELACE
(1618–1658)

Three golden coins are presented to you on a plate. One is romance, one is brotherly love, and the last is God's love. You can have them all. Which will you pick first?

Wait—before you make your decision, you should know that two of the coins have dark undersides. You can pick up pain as well as ecstasy with the first two coins, *eros* and *philos*. Only the third is exactly the same on both sides. That is the pure gold coin of *agape*, God's love for us; our sacrificial love for God.

God alone promises to love us now and forever:

Love never ends; as for prophecies, they will pass away; as for tongues, they will cease; as for knowledge, it will pass away.
—I Corinthians 13:8–13

Of the three coins of love, which was your first choice? If it was romance, you are in the majority. From the age of awakening to the age of senility, most of us are romantics within our secret hearts. To be the object of someone's admiration and desires, to be wanted and needed, to fill our arms, is a human craving as natural as the desire for food and water.

When God created man and woman, He raised us above His other creatures by giving us the ability to fall in love. He gave us brains that can imagine a future with our lovers, and even—God willing—an eternity together.

39

King Solomon, extolled for his wisdom, set down a prayer of thanksgiving for God's gift of all manifestations of love. Part of his "Song of Songs" captures the essence of being in love:

> Lord, I am a flower of Sharon, (fragrant to
>   my love)
> A lily of the valley. As a lily among thorns,
>   so is my beloved among women.
> As an apple tree among the trees of the wood,
> So is my beloved among the sons.
> I sat down under his shadow with great delight,
>   and his fruit was sweet to my taste.
> He brought me to the banqueting house, and
>   His banner over me was love.
> His countenance is as excellent as the cedars of
>   Lebanon,
> His mouth is most sweet.
> He is altogether lovely.
> This is my beloved, and this is my friend.
>   —ADAPTED FROM "THE SONG OF SONGS"

What a wonder is the coin of love called eros, filled as it is on the bright side with sexual energy and romantic yearning! It brings us more thrills, excitement, and promise than any other natural longing. Romantic love turns us into artists and poets, alive to beauty.

Although romance has taken a beating in our age of sexual freedom, it is far from dead. No matter what complications age may produce, very young lovers and very old lovers alike know that gestures of pure romance—a gentle touch, a lingering look, or a shared joke—are the jewels of happiness.

Choosing romantic love can be the pathway to loving friends, family, and even God more fully.

St. Augustine wrote a prayer of thanks to God for allowing him to taste of romance on his way to the celibate life.

Prayer of the Restless Heart

Almighty God, You have made us for Yourself, and our hearts are restless till they find their rest in You.

Our own restless hearts are the first source for understanding love's diversity. As we fall in love, we feel our hearts expand with love for things beyond the beloved just as ripples in water expand from a pebble.

Maybe it is because I fell in love with a very romantic man that I put so much faith in romance. Or maybe it is because I have had far longer than most people to contemplate the two sides of the coin of eros.

Before I was ten years old, an aunt paid our home an extended visit. She was a young woman who had been widowed for a little over a year. One day I found her crying, and she said, "Will anyone ever love me again?"

We stood there, a woman and a child, she holding both my hands in hers. It seemed a simple question. She believed I understood. But we were speaking different languages. Closing my eyes, I concentrated on love, as a child knows love, and I saw she would be surrounded by family throughout her lifetime, and that her two children would revere her in old age. I was very surprised to find she was still crying after all that good news.

She left me then, but a few days later she took my hands again and asked, "Jeane, will I ever be married again?" Once more I looked to the future and saw that, indeed, there would be a distinguished man linked to her in a circle of love that was different from her connection to all other people. And this time her smile told me that I had given her hope for the romantic love she craved.

Through the years I've heard countless questions about romantic love. I've been able to encourage many couples who went on together for years of happiness, but I have counseled just as many people to "get over it!" Finding romantic love is a serious, lifelong business.

No matter what other advice I might give, there is always this: The only three individuals whose opinions count are you, your beloved, and God.

In praying for love, we must be very willing to listen

for God's whispered answer. In committing ourself to a lover, a relationship, or a marriage, we are pledging years of our lives, our trust, and often our futures.

Before entering any relationship, we should pray for the signs that point to divine inspiration:

PRAYER FOR DIVINE INSPIRATION

Lord, let me hear Your voice clearly at this crossroads in my life.

If inspiration comes from You, I will never feel more truly alive.

If inspiration comes from You, my beloved's happiness will be my happiness.

If inspiration comes from You, there will be harmony in my heart and in my home.

If inspiration comes from You, I know my commitment will deepen.

If inspiration comes from You, I will seek and cling to truth and do what is right.

If inspiration comes from You, I will see beauty and feel charity in all things done with or for my love.

And, Lord, I know if I act on inspiration that comes from You, I will be made new. My life will never be the same. True love makes us new.

If there is ever a reason to listen in prayerful meditation for God's guidance, it is after our sincere prayer to find a person who needs us as much as we need him or her.

A Prayer for Someone with a Prayer Like Mine

Dear Lord, only You will understand my sadness and my hope. You Who know the recesses of our hearts know that my heart is breaking from loneliness.

I desperately want someone to care deeply about me and to let me care as much for them. I do have friends and family—and I thank You for all of them—but it is not the same as a romantic love.

Sometimes I am jealous of couples walking hand in hand. I fight envy, but I want a moment to share in their joy.

Confession is surely good for the soul. Indeed, even as I pray, Lord, You are helping me to see the bigger picture.

In that larger vision, You show me that romance often ends in sorrow, not happiness ever after. I begin to appreciate how You have sheltered me from hurts that may be worse than my loneliness. I can see that those whom I have en-

vied have their own burdens, different from mine, and perhaps far heavier.

Even in my hunger for a romantic glance, a loving touch, I feel You healing me in thought. You are telling me to search less for dreamy romance and more for the real people who need my concern. You are teaching me to lose my loneliness in the loneliness of others, especially those who are neglected by the world's frantic pursuit of happiness.

I accept Your call to a higher love, but never forget my prayer, please, Lord. I will always need that one companion that I can call mine alone. If it is Your will, let it be someone who is praying now, a prayer like mine.

⬩

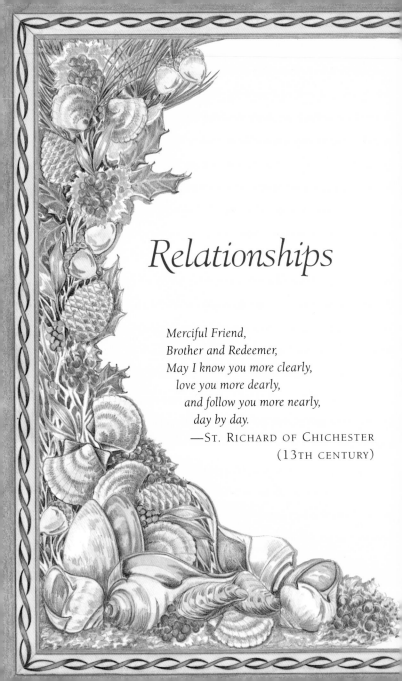

Relationships

Merciful Friend,
Brother and Redeemer,
May I know you more clearly,
  love you more dearly,
    and follow you more nearly,
      day by day.
        —St. Richard of Chichester
          (13th century)

Of all the relationships we enter into over the course of a lifetime, each of us has no more than a handful that are really important to our happiness. For these we should be thankful every day of our lives.

There are always three presences in Spirit-tied relationships—you, me, and God. With prayer, falling in love or finding a soul mate of any age or sex can grow into a spiritual relationship—indeed, friendship and love is *meant* to become spiritual. All good human relationships are exercises in expanding our capacity for the love of Him.

The pinnacle of human relationships is the blessing of a long-lasting marriage or deep friendship.

Love that endures blinds lovers' eyes to time's ravages.

For me, the best part of being in love with my husband for more than forty years was that we never saw each other aging. Whenever I looked at Jimmy Dixon I saw a young man in his prime, so anxious to have me that he slipped a ring from the dime store onto my finger rather than wait for the wedding rings we ordered from the jeweler.

And, on the last morning of his life, when he called my name, I know he was speaking to the girl inside me; the quicksilver girl that no one but he remembered.

The true gold of being in love, or having a friend of many years, is that someone knows your secret name; the name you answer to in dreams, where you remain forever young.

LET THERE ALWAYS BE
SOMEONE WHO KNOWS
MY NAME

*Your love, Lord, gives me everything I really
need. Why should I ask for more? The answer is
a dream You planted in my heart and soul. All
that I envision of Paradise came from You. You
bade me search and find the one lover born to
call me by my name.*

*Through all the years to come, let there be
someone whose eyes smile when I come into a
room. Let there be someone who needs to touch
my hand. Let there be someone who knows my
true name, the name You, in infinite knowledge,
called me from the beginning of time.*

*Lord, I need someone who will walk with me
in sunshine. But for the future, I need to know
that the same hand will be in mine if I am dis-
graced, dispirited, or in a hospital bed.*

*And let my heart always quicken in return.
For this kind of love must be matched, joy for
joy, desire for desire, openness for openness, sacrifice for sacrifice. Don't let me forget to say my
beloved's name with love, or surely our dream
will fade.*

❖

Everyone needs someone who sees them through the eyes of love. That special person can be a sister across the continent, or a friend who knows you need cheering by the tone of your voice, or someone you've worked beside for years and years. And for many of us, there is no warmer friend than the pet who rushes to the door at the sound of a key in the lock.

Chemistry, that instant spark of recognition when we meet certain people, is surprisingly accurate in predicting who will become our friends or lovers. We meet by chance, luck, or answered prayer. What happens next depends a great deal on, for want of a better word, fun.

Fun, laughter, shared adventures; these are the experiences that can turn ordinary relationships into friendship, and can turn friendship over time into filial or even romantic love.

So if each of us gets only a handful of meaningful relationships, how do we pick our precious few companions and lovers? How do they choose us?

My guess is that most people are instantly drawn to others who appear happy and to be having fun with their lives.

CONFESSION OF A FUN-LOVER

Lord, when I look back on all the treasured friends that have shared my life, I think first of the warmth of shared laughter and fun.

I confess I am attracted to beauty in men, women, children, flowers, animals, and every-thing else made by You or fashioned by man that is pleasing to the eye.

To do otherwise would be a rejection of Your infinite bounty. Thank You, Lord, for so much that is beautiful. Thank You for an eye that sees beauty in intelligence, beauty in humor, and beauty in the wisdom of my friends.

Friends tell me that you don't need to be psychic to guess whether someone is going to be important in your life. But I'm sure that my ability to pick up the vibrations of a stranger gives me an edge in finding true friends. There is, for instance, a great lady working with me to-day who was a teenager, an aspiring hairdresser when I met her thirty years ago. She took my advice and edu-cated herself for a business career. Another good friend is a powerful senator. Another is a man who changed his life in prison. Another is a widow with one of the great-est names in publishing, and the fortune that goes along with it.

The point is, don't turn off a possible friendship just because you cannot match wealth or position. All hu-man beings need friends who can see their needs be-neath the trappings of their place in God's great tapestry of life.

Prayer of Thankfulness
for Friends

Lord, I have been blessed beyond measure by the loving relationships You have given me. The friends You sent have shared grief and given comfort. They have shared their skills and wisdom, and the ones I hold dearest have laughed with me.

I believe that when I am happy, You, Lord, laugh with me, too.

As imperfect as my way has been, thanks to Your goodness, Lord, I have found true friends.

If my true friends, the people I love and who love me in return, were gathered in a room, it would be a small room. And the only person in the world who would think them all incomparably beautiful, or worthy, would be me. Among themselves they would look around in wonder that so many marginal characters had been invited to the party.

A relationship with another human being, like our relationship with God, is so unique that outsiders, however much they love us, never fully understand what we see in our friends, or what they see in us.

We may be attracted to relationships through unexplainable chemistry, but in the end we choose, and are chosen, because something in us is lovable. What makes us lovable is our ability and willingness to love another person.

HELP ME TURN MY LOVE
TO ACTION

Lord, give me the chance to do something wonderful for someone today. Let me gather enough love to give some away.

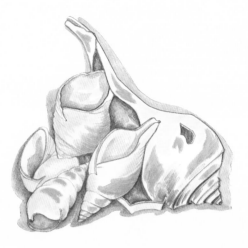

St. Francis of Assisi, so it was said, was ugly, small, and wizened by sacrificial living. Under the vow of poverty, he had nothing worldly to give. Legend has it that a very handsome monk envied Francis, and finally in frustration cried out, "Why you? Why do they all run after you?"

Francis replied, "Because I love them."

And St. Francis gave us a beautiful formula for becoming lovable:

THE ST. FRANCIS PRAYER

Lord, make me an instrument of Thy peace;
Where there is hatred, let me sow love;
Where there is injury, pardon;
Where there is doubt, faith;
Where there is despair, hope;
Where there is darkness, light;
And where there is sadness, joy.

O Divine Master, grant that I may not so much
seek to be consoled as to console;
To be understood as to understand;
To be loved, as to love;
For it is in giving that we receive,
It is in pardoning that we are pardoned, and it
is in dying that we are born to eternal life.

This goes to show that we don't need beauty, wealth, or power to be lovable. Of course, being lovable doesn't exclude any of these things. And certainly beauty, riches, and power can open many doors and make life a party while they last. They are just not enough to buy true friendship or true love.

Being lovable is like being in the good grace of God. For some of us, it's a constant struggle. At any point in life we can drift, harden our hearts because of disappointments or grief, and shut the door to life.

If we retreat from love, life, and social contacts, the world will let us fade away. If we complain about life, life will surely give us something to complain about.

Whether we choose it, or loneliness chooses us, few escape for a lifetime.

So where does the love come from if you are sitting alone finishing up your single-serving meal?

The first step is prayer. Praise God for the blessings of the people who have loved you; and the people who may, given the opportunity, love you still.

Listen for God to name someone to you. It could be a brother who did you wrong, but who longs for your forgiveness. It could be a child who feels too much guilt to make an overture after a long period of silence.

If necessary, count your enemies and you may find you have misjudged a friend.

WHO IS THE BROTHER
I AM TO LOVE?

Lord, who did You tell me to love when You said I must love my neighbor as myself? Tell me where to look, the place I must go, the scripture I must read, the charity that is required. I will listen quietly for Your voice. I will do as You bid me.

Perhaps the first step away from loneliness is to thank God, in prayer, for something in life that is unquestionably good. The sun can be turning rain into a rainbow outside our window, but if the shade is drawn tightly enough, it might as well be storming. Free will allows us to ignore God's love by hiding behind the shades of bitterness, heartbreak, and rejection.

Allowing God to love you through prayer is a giant step toward filial relationships. Pray for love. Pray for friendship. And pray for the good sense to recognize love or companionship when it is offered.

PRAYER FOR FRIENDS AND COMPANIONS

*Dear Lord, thank You for the faith Your love
    has built.*
*Keep my heart open, even when my arms are
    empty.*
*Let me recognize love when I see it, and not lose
    friendship while waiting for an ideal.*

As an anonymous poet once wrote:

*I believe in the sun, even when it is not shining. I
believe in love, even when I feel it not. I believe
in God, even when He is silent.*

For me, life wouldn't be complete without the animal friends who have shared my life. God must surely love the animals he created to be our companions on earth. He has counted every feather, the Bible tells us.

When Jesus instructed his apostles to teach, he did not say, "Preach the Gospel to every man," but "Preach the Gospel to every creature."

Cathedral builders took up the challenge. If you look at old-world cathedrals, you will see they are carved with trees, flowers, birds, fish, and other creatures made by God. There are cows carved at the top of the cathedral at Lyons and vegetables over the door of the cathedral at Rheims.

We must love God and our brothers first, but the love we show every creature, great and small, is certainly pleasing to the Lord.

In honor of my little dog and special friend, Capucine, here is a prayer for strays:

PRAYER OF A STRAY

Dear God, please send me somebody who will care. I'm tired of running. I'm sick with despair.

Dear God, I'm tired and hungry and cold. And I'm so afraid that I'll never grow old.

If You find me an owner, I'll try to be good. I won't chew their shoes. I'll do all that I should.

I'll love them, protect them, and try to obey when they tell me to sit, lie down, or to stay.

I've got so much love and devotion to give that I should be given a new chance to live.

❖

Lost Love

*It is only in adversity that we come
to know whether we have made
real progress in goodness.*
—St. Anthony of Padua
(1195–1231)

God knew what He was doing when He gave us our in-born hunger for human love, and the companionship of friends. Otherwise only the very brave or the very fool-ish would pursue it so fervently all their lives long.

The very word "companion" comes from root words that mean "with bread"—meaning that in addition to needing bread we also need someone with whom to share it. But human beings love us and leave us. And we leave them. This is the darker underside of the coins we call filial and romantic love.

Centuries pass but the rules of human relationships don't change. Read the sixth-century Greek tragedies, read Shakespeare, read yesterday's newspaper. People grow apart. Disagreements happen. Partnerships break. Arguments, divorce, illness, violence, and death threat-en human relationships from day one.

When partnerships break due to human frailty, the reason is probably that early in the relationship one or both of the individuals made a mistake or told a lie.

Most of us don't mean to lie to anyone, least of all to ourselves. But the need for love and companionship can knock the thinking process off base. And we must face the fact that some people do tell fibs in words and actions. The most common mistake is to believe yourself or a lover who says, "I'll love you forever . . . as much as I do today."

The only love that we cannot lose is God's love. Even lifelong friendships have low periods. But the more cen-tral God is to any relationship, the more faithful it is apt to be.

Thousands of young brides and grooms who swore eternal love on their wedding day never walk hand in hand into old age with their beloved. And behind faceless windows of every city, town, and farm are lonely people, who have lost or never found a true lover.

That is why marriage conducted by a clergyman is so important. Such marriages can and do fail, but when two truly prayerful people stand in the sight of God, with Him as a partner, the chance for establishing a loving family is greater, and is made manifest in the very air of the holy place where the ceremony takes place.

Whenever I get an invitation to a wedding, I hope and pray that God will be the guest of honor there.

INVITATION TO A WEDDING

Dear Lord, I have an invitation to a wedding. I'm excited because I'll see You there. Usually at weddings, You are everywhere I look.

You are on the altar with the clergyman. You are in the tears of the mothers and in the solemnity of the fathers. I see You in the eyes of other guests and the very air is perfumed with Your love.

We know, Lord, that You make marriages in heaven. But we also know that people make mistakes when they do not wait to hear Your benediction on their love.

Lord, how great You are to answer prayers for true love. How great You are to forgive mistakes and comfort the disappointed. How great You are to help us keep prayerful love alive. Thank You for coming to our weddings. Come early. Stay late. Never leave the banquet.

We've all been to weddings where God's absence is felt.

There are people who intend to clean up their acts after they get married—no more drugs, binges, affairs. If their intentions are truly good, God will be there.

There are couples who seem to be forming corporations rather than families. They prefer getting shares in mutual funds to getting table linens. I was a guest at one very stylish marriage that lasted less time than the couple spent living together before the wedding. They split the mutual fund; no hard feelings.

The danger is that physical attraction, or infatuation, can lead us into false relationships in which we may equate beauty with goodness and desire with love. False relationships are like pink spun-sugar candy—they look lovely and taste sweet. But without the substance of commitment, false relationships can make us sick. And as our bodies, minds, and spirits are all entwined, all three are put at risk. False love can bloat the ego without nourishing the soul.

Prayers to recognize true relationships needn't be long or poetic. I heard a very respected, and long-married, preacher—one who is noted for the fullness of his prayers—recite the prayer that sprang from his heart when he found himself falling in love with his wife. The prayer was richly answered with a wonderful marriage. He prayed: "Lord, don't let me make a mistake!"

Costly mistakes are not confined to romantic love. How many times do we break our hearts by rushing into friendship?

While he was a bishop in Poland, another great preacher, Pope John Paul II, prayed to God for caution in choosing companions and in accepting filial love:

MAN OF EMOTION

Between heart and heart there is always a gap.
You must enter it slowly—
'til the eye absorbs color,
the ear tunes to rhythm.
Love and move inward, discover your will,
shed heart's evasions and the mind's harsh
  control.

There is no use bemoaning the perils of love—not when the rewards are so wonderful, not when true love can be a taste of heaven on earth. But we must very faithfully pray our way into and through these relationships.

Falling out of love is only one of the ways we disappoint each other in relationships. Lapses in mental or physical health can turn partners into strangers. Financial and family problems call for unity that we may not feel. Whole books have been devoted to times when bad things happen to good people. I call these challenges "brown periods."

Just as a beautiful autumn dies to winter, sometimes our love also enters a brown period. In brown periods, we seem to be making no headway or slipping backward into sickness, job problems, or financial difficulties.

Several years ago, trying to adjust to life without my husband, I wrote a prayer for just this kind of situation:

PRAYER ON A BAD DAY

Dear Lord, this has not been a good day. So much has gone wrong for me. This is not the way I planned it at all. I do not want days like this, and I do not see why I have to live through them.

Wait a minute, please, Lord. Let me try to say that in a different way—because when I actually hear the words I have said to You, I am ashamed to be so ungrateful.

After all, it was You who gave me this day, and I really do appreciate Your giving it to me. Even more than that, You fill it with more blessings than I can count. I just overlook them sometimes, and take them for granted sometimes, and neglect them sometimes.

And sometimes, I just get so weary with the way things are going, with all the hurts and disappointments, that I fail to see, all around me in every aspect of the day, the evidence of Your care, compassion, and love.

I should remember that You, Lord, of all beings, have first-hand experience with bad days. Like the day Your friends deserted You when the Romans came to arrest You. And the day that

followed, when You suffered far worse things than I have to endure.

So You do know about my bad day, don't You? You know why I have been so low, so down, so troubled.

Just talking to You this way, Lord, makes my problems seem smaller. They may still be there, because You did not give me a magic wand to wave them all away. But You gave me something better—the assurance that You will always be with me, even to the end of time.

Knowing that, I can deal with whatever this day offers me. No matter how things turn out, win or lose, Your presence and love are going to make this a very good day.

The word "loneliness" is always associated with brown periods. We feel left out, overlooked.

I have felt this even in church! When I walk out after services, I pass groups of friends who are going off to breakfast. Families hurry to their cars and I envision them on the way to Grandma's house for Sunday dinner.

Sometimes, when I have sunk into gloomy prayer, I hear a shout that always brings a smile to my lips. It is from an Old Testament story about Moses. It seems that when Pharaoh gave the people permission to go from Egypt, God shouted to Moses: "Quit praying and get the people moving" (Exodus 14:15).

Then I know that God is with me and has given me

my marching orders to look around for someone else who needs a bit of encouragement. There always seems to be someone who looks a bit undernourished in body or spirit, and in offering some small service to that person, I am no longer alone.

Brown periods are times for us to be like nature. They can be little vacations of the spirit. Like nature's winter, brown periods are meant for shaking off dead branches and leaves in preparation for new growth.

Bitterness is another enemy of relationships and happiness. So too are revenge, wrath, greed, envy, gluttony, lust, and pride. Perhaps the worst crime against harmony among loving companions is failure to keep a friend or lover's confidence.

Who among us has not felt the sting of betrayal? Who among us in not guilty of the same mistake that destroys trust? Sometimes we decide we must get out of a relationship. A new friend or a new lover sweeps us away and we are the heartbreakers.

We are never needier of God's love than when, in honesty, we acknowledge that we have no one to blame but ourselves for lost love.

Conscience, if we would listen to it, tells us when we are at fault. Bishop Fulton J. Sheen wrote: "Unhappiness is often caused by disregarding our conscience. It is like singing a bad note, declaring it right, and tearing up the music sheet. There is no real happiness in tearing up the music or killing off our conscience. With God there is always a way back . . . just for sincere asking."

To apologize is one of the hardest things we can do. But through prayer, God will give us the strength we need to trade false pride for another chance at love.

PRAYER OF FORGIVENESS FOR FAILING IN LOVE

Dear Lord, my precious friend, You know that I am weak and weary. Conscience tells me I have done wrong to another. Pride keeps me from admitting my mistake. Show me how to make amends. Give me words and actions to apologize so fully that my love shines like new. If I must, help me to accept rejection gracefully. Let me keep my dignity through this sorry affair so that You, at least, will be proud to own me. You know my sorrows and my joys. Tell me what I ought to do, what I ought to try.

It may seem hard to believe, but I have found that as our life in prayer increases, we can actually lose our desire for human companionship. Biographies of saints tell the stories of many happy hermits. But saints are few and far between.

Even when we feel we have lost our hunger for love, lost our ability to love, lost the strength to be lovable, God still commands us to love others as we love Him. So we must pray for help to keep His commandment alive.

No Rest from Love

Lord, I want to be alone with You and only You for just a little while. Why must I always be called back by human needs? The phone rings, the mail needs response, the work day begins. I want to shut it all out. I want to stay here in peace with You.

You answer, "No, not yet."

You give me no permission to take a rest from loving. For as You love me, I must let the light flow through me to others. By loving me You give the example of love's bounty. Help me, then, to do as You command. Let me return love for love. Let me reach out to others.

✢

Hurting

I have a plan for your life,
it is a plan for good, not evil.
It is a plan to give you a future with hope.
—JEREMIAH 29:11

Being different hurts. Being persecuted or imprisoned hurts. All illnesses of body, mind, or spirit prevent us from enjoying benefits that others take for granted.

If you don't fit in at school or can't go to school at all, it hurts. If you are in a wheelchair while others are running, it hurts. If you can't get or hold a job because you are not considered "normal," it hurts.

No individual, no family, is free of sorrow. But in sorrow, mankind has always found comfort in God. A Psalmist wrote:

> *Incline your ear, O Lord; answer me, for I am af-*
> *flicted and poor.*
> *Keep my life, for I am devoted to you; save your*
> *servant who trusts in you.*
> . . . .
> *For you, O Lord, are good and forgiving,*
> *abounding in kindness to all who call upon*
> *you*
> *Hearken, O Lord, to my prayer and attend to*
> *the sound of my pleading.*
> *In the day of my distress I call upon you, for you*
> *will answer me.*
>
> —PSALM 86:1

❖

Loving someone who has been pushed out of life's mainstream is as painful, sometimes more so, as if it had happened to ourselves. In many cases we are powerless

71

to protect our child, our parent, or our loved one from the "slings and arrows of outrageous fortune."

What comfort can we find in prayer? The answer is that by praying we voice our hope and trust in God. Hope, trust, and faith are like the muscles of the spirit—the more we use them, the stronger they become.

In prayer we listen for God's instructions. Where should we go? What should we do? Who has the skill to change our condition? When should we make peace with ourselves? When should we give up one dream for another?

After we pray, how do we know the ideas that form in our minds come from God? One test of divine inspiration is in the confidence we feel when we act on His instruction. Other tests include feeling good about our actions, confidence in the sincerity of our motives, and knowing we are not hurting others in the process.

God seldom comes to us after prayer in any other voice but our own. A new thought enters our mind. We feel compelled to try again at something that has failed in the past.

Alexander Graham Bell loved and married a woman who was deaf. He wrote that when one door closes, another one opens, but we often look so long and so regretfully upon the closed door that we do not see the one that has opened for us. Sometimes a door closing on a loved one is harder to face than our own hurts.

Caring for someone who is ill, or giving hope to

the persecuted or imprisoned, are among God's highest callings.

Conscience tells us we are God's hands on earth. But not everyone is strong enough to care for, pray for, and love someone who is "different." While we may not be able to do the lifting and carrying, we can and should pray for our brothers and sisters.

Praying someone through rejection or infirmity is the mark of a truly prayerful person. God smiles when we pray for others. Those who are mature in spiritual life, like cloistered nuns and monks, spend the greater part of the day in prayers of intercession—often for strangers.

For centuries, people have comforted themselves with this prayer for the afflicted:

Prayer of Hope for the Suffering

Sovereign Lord, our God Almighty, we beseech You to save us all; You, the only Physician of souls and bodies, minds and spirits. Sanctify us all, You who healest every disease; and heal also this Your servant.

Raise him up from the bed of pain by Your tender mercy and compassion; drive away from him all sickness and infirmity; that being raised by Your almighty hand, he may serve You with all thankfulness; and that we may be made par-

takers of Your unspeakable kindness, may praise and glorify You, who perform works great and wonderful, and worthy to be praised.

For it is Yours to pity and to save; and to You we ascribe glory, Father, Son, and Holy Spirit, now and forever, and unto ages of ages. Amen.

One of the loveliest stories I ever heard involved a mother who saved pennies for years to take her severely retarded daughter to Lourdes. Since the child could not walk on her own, both child and mother entered the water. The mother returned to her home confused by her own feelings. Although her daughter was the same as always, a happy child, well loved by her family, the mother was changed. Her miracle was acceptance.

Some may say there was no miracle of healing for the mother who took her daughter to Lourdes. I disagree. Miracles seldom come with claps of thunder.

Direct miracles must be treasured as the rarest of jewels. In our hearts we know that God, no matter how much He loves us, never promised He would go against nature. To make us more than human is not one of God's promises.

The evidence of this is the life and death of Christ, who suffered all these things while assuming his humanity. The evidence is also in Mary, the mother who grieved. And yet Christ prayed, as we should, "thy will be done."

Bad things do happen to good people. Take comfort in the Old Testament story of Job, who was richly blessed and then cruelly tormented. In his lamentations, Job wrote the book on human suffering.

Job's Lament

Lord, I am brought to nothing; as a wind thou hast taken away my desire; and my prosperity hath passed away like a cloud.

And now my soul fadeth within myself, and the days of affliction possess me.

I cry to thee, and thou hearest me not: I stand, and thou dost not regard me.

Thou hast lifted me up, and set me as it were upon the wind, and thou hast mightily dashed me.

I know that thou wilt deliver me to death, where a house is appointed for everyone that liveth.

—Book of Job

✥

There is no doubt that Job was angry at God. But, despite his anger, he knew that God must love him still—even in silence. Job found comfort in his angry prayer, and in the end God rewarded Job's patience and restored his health.

Psychiatrists tell us that it is good for us to lay out our troubles, have a look at them, and weigh them against the human condition. We realize then that while some people are better off than we are, there are others in even worse pain. It is of some comfort to know that we are not alone.

Illness, which comes to us all, cuts all of us out of the mainstream of life for short or long periods. Recently, I suffered a rather long illness and wrote this prayer . . . and in His goodness, God brought me back:

Prayer in Time of Illness

Dear Lord, over the centuries, You have been called the Divine Physician of Souls. Well, today I come to You for physical, spiritual, and emotional healing.

In ancient Israel there was a woman who believed that if she could only touch the hem of Your garment she would be cured of her affliction.

You made her well, dear Lord, as You healed so many others of their illnesses. You did so not

76

only to show Your divine power, but most of all because You loved them.

You loved them as individuals, with all their faults and failings, just as You love me. And so I know that, even in my illness, You keep me in Your care.

I want to get well, and quickly. Help me to do all I should do to recover.

Sometimes it is hard to be a good patient. Help me to try harder to be that.

Help me remember those whose burdens are heavier than mine, especially those who, in their sickness, do not know of Your love and saving grace.

And if it is not Your will that I should recover soon, teach me happiness even in loss, and joy even in pain.

When You healed the ten lepers, only one returned to thank You. Let me always be like him, full of gratitude for what You have done for me—and full of hope for the new life You teach me to live.

One of the divine mysteries is why some are persecuted and others live lives that seem to outsiders to be free of care. Comfort lies in knowing we are all children of God.

Prayer of the Persecuted

Dear Lord, no matter how I look to others,
    I thank You for myself. You created no
    mistakes.
I may be young; I may be old,
But I am somebody, for I am Your Child.
I may be educated, I may be unlettered,
But I m somebody, for I am Your Child.
I may be black; I may be white,
But I am somebody, for I am Your Child.
I may be rich; I may be poor,
I may be fat; I may be thin,
I may be married; I may be divorced,
I may be successful; I may be a failure,
I may be a sinner, I may be a saint,
But I am somebody, for I am Your Child.

—BASED ON A POEM BY
AN UNKNOWN AUTHOR

Although I have never been arrested, I am no stranger to Lorton prison, which stands outside of Washington, D.C. Some of my oldest friends were once behind bars there, and I am proud to say that I have helped a few of them find their way back. The bars of a prison cannot keep God from men of faith.

One of the world's greatest prayers was written by a

man who spent most of his adult life in prison. For forty years, Baha'u'llah, whom the Baha'i faithful call The Messenger of God, lived behind bars in exile until his death in 1892.

You Heal Me with Your Name

Thy name is my healing, O my God, and remembrance of Thee is my remedy. Nearness to Thee is my hope, and love for Thee is my companion. Thy mercy to me is my healing and my succour in both this world and the world to come. Thou, verily, art the All-Bountiful, the All-Knowing, the All-Wise.

Does God love the "different" among us? Does he comfort us in our pain? Yes, and yes again.

But is some kind of suffering the way to insure God's love? No! God takes no pleasure in, has no need of our pain. He wants us to be happy, as we want those we love to be happy.

Twelve Steps to Mystic Prayer

Truth is what prays in man, and man is continually at prayer when he lives according to truth.

—EMMANUEL SWEDENBOURG (1688–1772)

I remember Saturday nights in my childhood when I would get into a tub of hot water to be scrubbed for church and the week ahead.

Now I get out my mental washboard to scrub away the pressures and mistakes of daily life, and to prepare myself for my favorite time of the week, when switchboards go quiet and the parade of humanity at my door marches away for the weekend's rest.

My rest is in prayer and meditation. My yearning is to have the solitude to reach for yet a third level of worship that lies beyond daily prayer and meditation. That place beyond is mystic prayer.

While there is always a time and a place for daily prayer, and a moment or two to listen for inspiration, there is seldom time to go farther. Sometimes we are left unsatisfied. Some level of our consciousness anticipates something more. It's as if love is just around the corner, but we must hurry off in a different direction.

Extended meditation allows us time to wait for a special meeting. It frees the spirit to roam. When I meditate for long periods, I seem to be able to hear with other ears and see with other eyes.

Extended meditation is a pathway to mystic prayer. People who devote their lives to prayer may travel the path to mystic prayer more often and more easily than the rest of us, but mystic prayer is not reserved for saints alone. Love and longing for God is our admission to the gateway to heaven.

To get there requires total surrender to God. In surrender, we literally forget who we are; we forget pain. We want nothing but to be the receptacle of God's love.

Although daily prayer and meditation confer enormous benefits, mystic prayer is a step into ecstasy.

While daily prayer is bread, the staff of life, deep meditation is like cake to most people—something to be desired but saved for special occasions. Beyond meditation, mystic prayer is the frosting on the cake, desired by those who would rather pray than eat.

When God wills it, meditation acts as a "bridge" between daily prayer, which comes from the mind and heart, and mystic prayer, which is spirit-driven. In mystic prayer, a higher power embraces and directs the spirit within us.

Intuition tells me that many people around the world know the ecstasy of praying in the spirit. Many more, I would guess, get close but pull back, afraid to step away from solid ground. You can be ready to take the leap of spirit at any age—or never feel the desire. Mystic prayer is not for everyone. Even among cloistered monks and nuns, I am told, mystic prayer is elusive.

Many people have wondered how I pray and meditate. On reflection, I can pinpoint twelve steps that are usually part of my ritual.

Do not think that I always have the solitude, the strength, or the will to progress through all twelve steps. Nor am I guaranteed the joy of mystic prayer even if I reach deep meditation. But no matter how far I go, nothing is lost, and much has been gained. Each step brings its own reward, the least of which is rest and refreshment of the body and mind.

Then there are those rare occasions when something wonderful happens. At any time in the cycle of prayer and meditation, you can soar into mystic prayer.

God can step in at any point to take you away. No meeting of friends is ruled by strict convention. Whenever love envelops you, the connection is complete, and there is no need for more preparation. No two encounters with God in prayer are exactly the same.

STEP 1

Prepare your body for sacramental prayer, first by bathing and then by getting into clothing that causes no distractions. Get into a comfortable, prayerful! position. You want every part of your body to be a closed circuit except the mind. Your feet should be on the floor or ground, and your fingers should be touching as they were when you were taught to pray as a child.

STEP 2

Ward off evil. I mean that literally. You must have God's protection before you attempt mystic prayer. For me, the most powerful line of the Lord's Prayer is "Deliver us from evil." The devil is at the door every day. Every day we should pray for protection from him—especially as we prepare for deep meditation.

83

Prayer for Deliverance from Evil

Deliver us, Lord, from every evil,
And grant us peace in our day.
In Your mercy keep us free from sin
And protect us from all anxiety
As we wait in joyful hope
For the coming of our savior.

✥

Step 3

Bid your senses to come alive by focusing on a stained-glass window or anything beautiful to the sight, and listening to the sounds of silence.

Step 4

Say a detoxification prayer, a calming prayer—a prayer that prepares the mind to become open and childlike, such as this one by George Appleton, Archbishop of Jerusalem (1902–1993):

The Heart of a Child

Grant me, O God, the heart of a child,
Pure and transparent as a spring;
A simple heart, which never harbors sorrows;
A heart glorious in self-giving,
Tender in compassion;
A heart faithful and generous
Which will never forget any good
Or bear a grudge for any evil.

✣

Step 5

Greet and acknowledge God. Praise Him with words, then be silent, letting your spirit worship the Lord on its own level. Send out your love.

Prayer of Adoration

O God, our God,
How glorious is Your name over all the earth!
Your glory is praised in the heavens.
Out of the mouths of children and babes
You have fashioned praise
To silence the enemy and the rebellious ones.
When I look at Your heavens, the work of Your
Hands, the moon and the stars, which You
    created—who are we that You should be
    mindful
Of us, that You should care for us?

You made us little less than the angels
And crowned us with glory and honor.
You have given us rule over the works of Your
Hands, putting all things under our feet.

Alternatively, this simple prayer of praise will do:

God, how glorious is Your name over all the
earth! You are great and I am small, but I love
You with every fiber of my being.

Step 6

Examine your conscience. Get rid of convenient lies. As excuses spring to mind, and they will, reject all that is not perfectly true. As Martin Luther warned us: "Don't lie to God!" Our hearts, minds, and intentions are clear as glass to God, but they are not always as clear to us— especially when desire goes against conscience.

Step 7

Confess your sins. Speak out loud if you are alone to claim the full spiritual value of confession. Acknowledge the specific acts that make you feel sinful. End with a general confession that asks forgiveness. To fail in this may lead you to judge yourself unworthy, and that can keep you from your goal of mystic prayer.

Confession

I confess to Almighty God that I have sinned in thought and deed, in what I have done and what I have failed to do. I ask You to forgive me, Lord, and help my brothers and sisters to forgive me as You do.

Step 8

Pray for your needs. Ask of God what you desire in the way of worldly things—love, friendship, security, or freedom from pain. Perhaps saints can refrain from asking the Lord to relieve suffering, but the rest of us must free our minds of distress before we can hope to clear the way for deep meditation.

Step 9

Raise your prayer to a higher level by saying prayers of intercession for others. Pray for the needs of family, friends, and society as a whole.

As we see the needs of the larger world, our prayers will turn outward in ever-widening circles. Pray for comfort for those who know fear. Pray for God to feed His hungry people. Pray for peace in the world.

Again, do not lie to God. Pray for universal intercession only when you truly feel love for mankind.

Prayer of Intercession

What can I do today to help the world? Lord, You need my hands to do Your work. I need Your inspiration to know where to start. Lord, feed Your people who are hungry in mind and spirit. Help us choose peace over war.

Step 10

Quiet the mind for meditation. This is so easily said and so difficult to do. Desires and transgressions are hard to get out of the mind. If they push back into your consciousness, drive them away with a prayerful mantra.

A mantra is a short prayer that is helpful in quieting the mind. Some people believe that silent repetition of a seven-syllable prayer like "Creator, show me Your love" makes a perfect mantra. "My Lord and my God" is a five-syllable mantra that works for others. The specific words are a personal choice. What is important is that the words focus the mind on the divine, driving away distracting thoughts.

Repeating any one of the beautiful lines of "Christ Be Beside Me" can also be a powerful mantra.

CHRIST BE BESIDE ME

Christ be beside me, Christ be before me.
Christ be behind me, King of my heart.
Christ be within me, Christ be below me.
Christ be above me, never to part.

Christ on my right hand, Christ on my left
*   hand.*
Christ all around me, shield in the strife.
Christ in my sleeping, Christ in my sitting,
Christ in my rising, Light of my life.

Christ be in all hearts thinking about me,
Christ be on all tongues telling of me.
Christ be the vision in eyes that see me.
In ears that hear me, Christ ever be.
> —St. Patrick (5th century)

Now you are on the brink of deep mediation.

STEP 11

Surrender your mind, will, and heart to God. Let go, and let God in. Listen and feel, don't think. If the mind wanders, go back to your mantra, repeating it until you are peaceful again. Perhaps then the communion with God that you seek will begin. Feel God's embrace in a way that only you can experience.

In this state of happiness with the Lord, I sometimes leave my body and soar to heavenly places. In contemplating God, I can see loved ones who are gone from earth but who still live in God and in my memory. Usually the mind cannot hold what is essentially an experience of the spirit. How long it lasts varies. The end is usually peaceful sleep.

Well . . . not always. Everyone has dry periods—brown periods, I call them. Julian of Norwich, a fourteenth-century saint who spent her life in contemplative prayer, described her dry periods thus:

Often we are as barren and dry after our prayers as we were before. And thus when we feel so, it is our folly. And our Lord brought all this suddenly to my mind, and revealed these words and said: "Pray wholeheartedly, though it seems to you that this has no savor for you; still it is profitable enough, though you may not feel that. Pray wholeheartedly, though you feel nothing, yes, though you think that you could not, for in dryness and in barrenness, in sickness and in weakness, then is your prayer most pleasing to me."

❖

If my meditations end without the joy of mystic prayer, as they often do, I am disappointed, but not in despair. The promise of Julian's vision is that God has heard me, and wants me to go on seeking Him in mystic prayer. God told her to pray even when she felt nothing . . . when she was barren, sick, and weak.

And so must we pray our way through brown periods with a prayer of acceptance.

Give Me Some Comfort, Lord

Give me some comfort, Lord. Just a ray of light will do. You are the ground of my beseeching. You willed me to meet You in prayer. You gave me the wish. You taught me to pray. I believe that You are answering in nothingness. Tell me what the nothingness means.

Step 12

Finally, say a prayer of thanksgiving, and promise to be a better person.

Whether or not we cross the "bridge" of deep meditation to that place where God is everything, we have prayed with power and purpose. And if we have been lucky enough to achieve mystic prayer, we have been granted the greatest of spiritual gifts.

Psalm 103

Bless the Lord, my soul:
    Lord, my God, You are truly magnificent!
You are arrayed in beauty and majesty,
    Clothed with Light as with a garment.
. . . .

Man goes forth to his work
    And to his toil until evening.
How Your works are multiplied, Lord!
    You have made all things with wisdom,
    The earth is full of Your creations.
. . . .

Send out Your spirit, and they will be created,
    And You will renew the face of the earth.
Let there be glory to the Lord forever;
    The Lord rejoices in His works.
. . . .

I will sing to the Lord all my life,
    I will sing a song to my God as long as I
        live.
May my speech be pleasing to Him,
    As for me, I will rejoice in the Lord.

Visions

In cases which concern private revelations, it is better to believe than not to believe, for if you believe, and it is proven true, you will be happy that you believed.

—POPE URBAN VIII
(1623–44)

Let me tell you about a vision I had about twenty years ago . . . a vision that led directly to the gathering of the prayers I share with you in this book.

I was awakened in our Washington, D.C., townhouse about 3 A.M. by the sweet scent of roses. As I followed the fragrance to a nearby window, I heard a voice that said, "Follow me." It was a voice I had heard before, and an instruction that I dared not turn from.

Before I knew it, I felt myself leaving our home and then the city altogether. Soon I found myself at the peak of a great mountaintop. Nearby was a golden cave and the same voice said, "Enter."

Inside was a golden throne, radiating with a color so stunning that it resembled a cloud when the sun moves behind it.

As I looked at the throne, the voice said to me, "Clothe yourself." I looked down and discovered I was naked.

"I have called you again," the voice reminded me. I remembered another time, early in my life of prophecy, when this had occurred. Then, as I reached behind what seemed to be a brick wall, I found a simple brown cloth to cover myself with. As I put it on, a brilliant, golden medallion fell over my heart.

When this happened, I felt a warm embrace, a love coming not just toward me, but from me. Then I heard the voice say, "This is how I manifest my life!"

At that point, love poured out of me so strongly that I feared I might dissolve. But what happened instead

95

was a marvelous realization: The more love I could give out, the more love could radiate through every part of my being and through every part of my soul—the more love could rush back to me. I knew then that this was the message of my journey: the love we give generates, in turn, the love we receive.

The voice of my host then said I must go, and what I heard from him was an instruction. He said, "You must leave me, and take to the world the manifestation of my life."

And that manifestation was the love that I saw and felt . . . the love all of us should send out.

Soon I found myself in front of our townhouse again, but dressed in a most spectacular way. I was wearing the clothing of an American Indian, which was the same brilliant golden color I saw on the mountaintop. From head to moccasin, I felt I was beaming, actually shining, through the golden clothes. And I was reminded of the vast knowledge that Indians have of life and all its mysteries. I was reminded that their reverence for the earth and its hidden beauties is truly the gold of our past, just as our natural resources will be the gold of our future.

When I awakened at home again, I knew the purpose of my journey was to leave the mountain as I was instructed to do, and to tell all who would listen that God is constant love.

Many people are given such visions, but most of them go unreported.

The sharing of visions can be a dangerous business today, no less than it has been throughout history. "Kill the messenger" was a time-honored way for despots to deal with bad news. Visions, unfortunately, are usually bad news for the rich and powerful, who often have been told to change their ways to please the Lord.

Those who get psychic messages in dreams or meditation are no more worthy, spiritual, or contemplative than those who do not. The great contemplative St. John of the Cross was able to read people's thoughts and was credited with healing powers. Yet, the eighteenth-century Franciscan, who foretold the date of his own death, rejected visions as self-serving and self-generated.

But I have been receiving visions, some prophetic, all my life. With some prophetic visions comes the command to make them known. The courage to do so comes from the history of prophecy. Time separates the true from the false. The few prophets recorded in ancient scripture were surely not alone among men in believing they had visions from God.

Those who survived the test of time somehow perceived more than the experience of their daily life could offer.

How could Isaiah, for example, who lived in a very brutal age, know that God is love unless he felt it for himself?

Isaiah is considered the greatest of the ancient prophets by many biblical scholars. He lived in the eighth century B.C., at a critical moment in history when the Chosen People were under attack from powerful enemies.

Isaiah had a vision of God on a lofty throne surrounded by angels who were singing his praises. At that moment Isaiah recognized his own sinfulness and specifically realized that he was misusing his gift of speech. Overcome with remorse, he cried out: "Woe is me, I am doomed. For I am a man of unclean lips" (Isaiah 6:5).

Then, in Isaiah's vision, an angel came down with a glowing ember and touched his lips, telling Isaiah, "Your sin [is] purged" (Isaiah 6:7).

Then in the vision, Isaiah heard the voice of the Lord saying, "Whom shall I send? Who will go for us?" "Here I am," Isaiah said; "send me!" And God replied: "Go and say to this people: 'Listen carefully, but you shall not understand! Look intently, but you shall know nothing!'" (Isaiah 6:8–10).

And thereafter the former sinner spoke well for the Lord, preaching this message: "Fear thou not; for I am with thee: Be not dismayed: for I am thy God: I will strengthen thee; yea, I will help thee; yea, I will uphold thee with the right hand of my righteousness" (Isaiah 41:10).

The answer to why one person out of a thousand is chosen for visions may be found in Isaiah's prayer.

It may be that only one out of a thousand is willing to say: "Send me!"

Of all the visionaries who have witnessed God's love, my personal favorite is Julian of Norwich, whose meditations on "brown periods" are helpful to me in achieving mystic prayer (see page 91). She was an Englishwoman, educated by nuns, who lived in the fourteenth century. Like me, she lived in the heart of a bustling city, worked as well as prayed, and recorded her revelations in a book.

The similarities stop there, for Julian was a mystic and theologian of the highest order. Her spiritual legacy began at age thirty, when, as she lay deathly ill, God entrusted her with sixteen revelations. She understood that these visions were "shown for all men," and that she was to publish them. Therefore, when she wrote down her visions, she called her book *Showings*.

In it she wrote:

> *God is everything which is good, as I see, and the goodness which everything has is God.*
>
> *God showed me this in the first vision, and he gave me space and time to contemplate it. And then the bodily vision ceased, and the spiritual vision persisted in my understanding. And I waited with reverent fear, rejoicing in what I saw and wishing, as much as I dared, to see more, if that were God's will, or to see the same vision for a longer time.*

Miraculously cured of her illness, the holy woman renounced whatever life she had known before this mystic experience. Some scholars believe she was a nun because she could read and write, but there is no record of her youth or even of her birth name.

To insure that she would have the solitude necessary to contemplate and impart her visions, Julian chose the life of a holy hermit. She was appointed Anchoress of St. Julian's, a busy parish in the city of Norwich, England. As was the custom, she took the name of her church, becoming Dame Julian.

There Dame Julian lived out her life alone in a room no larger than ten feet square. One window of her room opened onto the altar of the church so she could participate in daily mass. The other opened onto a public road, so that passersby could seek her counsel simply by knocking on her shutter. There, she wrote *Showings*.

The date of her death was never recorded, but from a book written by a visitor to her cell in 1413, we know Julian lived a long and respected life.

That visitor was another outstanding churchwoman, Margery Kempe, an early evangelist. To Kempe, Julian emphasized the message of God's love.

Kempe wrote: "The anchoress, hearing the marvelous goodness of Our Lord, highly thanked God with all her heart for his visitation."

Kempe quoted the anchoress as saying: "The Holy Ghost moveth ne'er a thing against charity, for if He did, He would be contrary to His own self for he is all charity."

Prayer of Julian of Norwich

God, of Your goodness,
Give me Yourself,
For You are enough for me, and
I can ask for nothing less which can pay You
Full worship.
And if I ask for anything less always I am
In want;
But only in You do I have everything.

Two hundred years later, another woman of vision, St. Teresa of Avila (1515–1582), wrote a similar prayer, which I think makes a fitting ending for this book:

Let nothing disturb you,
nothing cause you fear;
All things pass
God is unchanging.
Patience obtains all:
Whoever has God
Needs nothing else,
God alone suffices.